Credit Repair Secrets

Discover the strategies to solve your debt and improve your score.

Table of contents

DISCOVER THE STRATEGIES TO SOLVE YOUR DEBT AND
IMPROVE YOUR SCORE. 1

INTRODUCTION..7

CHAPTER 1: BASICS OF CREDIT REPAIR 8
WHAT IS CREDIT REPAIR? 10
HOW CREDIT REPAIR WORKS..12

CHAPTER 2: GOOD OR BAD RATING 13
720 AND ABOVE—EXCELLENT..14
680–719—GOOD 14
620–679—AVERAGE 15
580–619—POOR 15
500–579—BAD...16
LESS THAN 500 16

CHAPTER 3: HOW TO REMOVE MISTAKES FROM CREDIT
REPORT 22
INITIATE A DISPUTE...22
CONTACT INFO FOR THE CRAS 23
WHAT HAPPENS AFTER YOU SUBMIT YOUR DISPUTE 24
WHEN THE CRA DOES NOT RESPOND TO YOUR DISPUTE.............................25

CHAPTER 4: CREDIT SCORE 31
THE FICO SCORING MODEL 31
HOW IS MY FICO SCORE CALCULATED? 34
HOW DO YOU CHECK YOUR CREDIT SCORE..36
WHAT IS A FICO SCORE?...38
WHAT IS A GOOD CREDIT SCORE? HOW CAN I IMPROVE MY CREDIT RATING
AND CREDIT SCORE? 40

CHAPTER 5: THE CRAS: GENERAL NOTIONS 42
ORIGIN AND HISTORY OF CRAS..43
WHAT DO CRAS DO? 45

CHAPTER 6: EFFECTIVE STRATEGIES FOR REPAIRING YOUR
CREDIT 50

PAY-TO-DELETE STRATEGY...50
CHECK FOR FDCPA (FAIR DEBT COLLECTION PRACTICES ACT) VIOLATIONS 53
REQUEST PROOF OF THE ORIGINAL DEBT...56

CHAPTER 7: WHAT IS CREDIT COUNSELLING? 58

WHEN IS IT TIME TO SEEK COUNSELING 60
HOME EQUITY LINE OF CREDIT (HELOC) 62
CREDIT BUILDER LOANS 63
FICO SCORES IMAGE 64
RATING AGENCIES...65

**CHAPTER 8: GUARANTEED METHODS TO PROTECT CREDIT
SCORE...67**

CHAPTER 9: FCRA AND SECTION 609 70

**CHAPTER 10: HOW TO WRITE A CREDIT REPAIR LETTER 609
....77**

GENERAL ADVICE TO SEE SUCCESS WITH 609 77
WHAT DO I INCLUDE IN MY CREDIT DISPUTE LETTER?.................85
OTHER LETTER TEMPLATES...93

CHAPTER 11: WHAT ARE MY RIGHTS UNDER 609? 103

CHAPTER 12: DEBT SNOWBALL 105

CHAPTER 13: HOW TO PAY DOWN DEBT 111

STOP WITH THE NEW DEBT...111
RANK THE DEBT USING INTEREST RATES 112
SEE IF YOU CAN LOWER INTEREST RATES 113
CREATE YOUR OWN BUDGET 114
CREATE YOUR OWN REPAYMENT SCHEDULE...............................115
BE KIND TO YOURSELF 116

CHAPTER 14: WHAT IS A CREDIT SCORE? 118

BENEFITS OF A GOOD CREDIT SCORE 119
THE FIVE STEPS TO ORDER A CREDIT REPORT 122

**CHAPTER 15: HOW TO BOOST YOUR CREDIT SCORE OF 100 POINTS
....126**

QUICK TIPS FOR REPAIRING YOUR CREDIT 128

CONCLUSION...134

INTRODUCTION

It's simple: Credit is your credibility as related to your name and social security number. Your credibility is built from your own financial borrowing patterns. You can develop creditability within any nation, organization, company, or with an individual, but being financially credible as we know it comes from our dealings with lenders, banks, and other forms of financial institutions. These financial entities furnish our information to credit reporting agencies and companies that import and then summarize our activities into algorithms, which they use to generate credit scores. These credit reporting agencies — abbreviated CRAs and also referred to as credit bureaus, credit reporting bureaus, consumer reporting agencies, or credit reference agencies — are corporations that store our information in a file to identify our past and current creditability but more importantly, they determine our future creditworthiness. Your past behavior will dictate your current credit standing or whether you can be trusted to borrow a small sum and pay it back on set terms, and if you can, you will then become more credible. It's that simple.

Chapter 1: Basics of Credit Repair

It is hard to navigate today's society using credit. A variety of companies use your credit history to place the pricing for services and goods you use and also whether to do business. Consumers with bad credit histories seek out credit repairs to increase their credit rates.

What Is Bad Credit?

Bad credit is when you have missed one or more payments throughout your life, be it your fault or not. The most common mistake people make is not defaulting on a payment, it is actually delaying payments. It is usually when you forget about a deadline or can't find a certain bill that makes you end up not paying, or being late; however, in the eyes of the people, borrowing money makes you look a bit financially unstable. Sometimes, even if you have had impeccable behavior, you are unfortunately affected by the loss of a job. Becoming unemployed has such grave consequences that can lead to your assets being repossessed or even bankruptcy. Even if you went through a similar phase and you have bounced back, having this kind of history will impact your credit report in a negative way for a very long period of time.

It can also happen to you to be the victim of an error, even if you have not missed a single payment on your credit card until now. An error in the bank's system or the parties responsible for building your credit report will affect you nonetheless, and so will fraud and abuse. Fraud cases are rare, but their consequences are costly. Fraud happens when someone uses your identity to submit a credit application—they get it, and then they do not repay it anymore. You will be contacted by the bank, and until you can prove you have been the target of a scam, you can have a tough time. Abuse generally refers to the times when you are oblivious of your expenses and keep spending over your credit card limit. You can wake up one day with a huge amount of debt, and cases of abuse most often end in you being forced to declare bankruptcy. In order to avoid these cases, you need to be very careful with your finances, but regardless of what your situation is, usually, there is a solution or a set of measures you can enforce to prevent it.

How to Avoid Bad Credit?

First of all, if you have lost your main source of income and are not able to make your payments in time or at all, it is important you say so. Announcing the fact that you may be unable to pay in the following months might land you a grace period from the lender. That means that you will not suffer any penalties for a given period of time. It is until you can get back on your feet, and maybe get a new job that you can resume your normal payments.

You have to prioritize bills, meaning you will have to make a few judgment calls on what bills you should pay with the money you have left, and which ones might be less likely to affect your credit. Keeping up with your bills is difficult, but it is also important if you do not want to end up with bad credit. Use your savings or whatever else you have available and you may be able to make your credit look good even if you went through losing your job. These methods work to prevent lack of credibility, but they also apply in the case of you doing damage control. A credit repair will be a lot easier if you benefit from a grace period and do not have as many overdue bills. It shows you were concerned and aware of the situation, and that you tried your best to remain in control of your finances.

What Is Credit Repair?

Credit repair is the process in which credit standing is fixed, which might have declined due to various reasons. Credit repair might be as straightforward as disputing the information in the credit report.

Another kind of credit repair is to take care of financial problems such as budgeting and start to deal with concerns.

Significant points to consider:

- Credit repair is the action of repairing or restoring a bad credit rating.
- Credit repair may also entail paying a company to get in touch with the credit reporting agency and point out anything in your report that is untrue or incorrect, then requesting this to be eliminated.

You can do your own credit repair, but it may be time-consuming and hard.

How Credit Repair Works

Though companies claim they are able to clean up credit reports that are poor, correcting requires time and energy. A third party cannot remove the information. The specifics, incorrect or misrepresented, can be contested. Individuals are eligible for free credit reports every 12 months in addition to if an action is taken against them. Disputes may be registered if incorrect or incomplete information appears in their credit reports. Besides correcting such errors, or discovering fraudulent trades on one's credit, fixing and rebuilding a credit report may break more heavily on credit use and credit action. The payment history of this person may be a factor in their own credit standing. Taking measures to make certain payments and current or enhance the payment program for outstanding credit may negatively impact their credit rating. The total amount of credit may play a role. As an example, if somebody is actively using huge parts of the credit available to them, even if they are keeping minimum payments in time, how much the debt they are taking on could negatively affect their credit score. The matter is that their liquidity might be driven by debt. They could see improvements by taking steps to decrease their debt burden.

Chapter 2: Good or Bad Rating

In a nutshell, your credit score could range from anywhere between the low 300s to the mid-800s. These are the general score ranges that are considered by CRAs and credit companies. It should be apparent from this that the 800 mark is the highest, and the 300 is the lowest.

As you already know, having a poor credit score will determine how much it costs you to access credit. The lower that it gets, the worse your interest rates and the more money you spend; however, we looked at how companies will flock to target you and try and get as much money out of you as possible. These figures are set based on calculations that are done by the CRAs. Depending on your credit history, they will add up your debts and come up with a number that will help determine where you stand.

To help you understand the scores better, here is a breakdown of the credit score ranges and what each means. You might probably find that your credit score is pretty bad than you thought!

720 and above—Excellent

When you have this score, you get the best interest rates and repayment terms for all loans. This score can come in handy if you are hoping to make some major purchases. You will avail yourself of credits without any problems and at the lowest possible rates. But then, this score is extremely hard to establish. You will have to put in a lot of effort to maintain this core and still, you will not come anywhere close to 800. The most you can wish is to come close to 720 and remain there for as long as possible.

680–719—Good

When you are in this category, you will get good rates and terms, but not as good as those with excellent scores. With this score, you can get favorable mortgage terms. You might not face as many problems but will have to be ready to run around from company to company to have your credit approved. Again, this score is not very common. You need to put in extra effort to get it over the 680 marks. If because of some erroneous charges you are not able to cross this limit, then you must try your best to get it cleared as soon as possible.

620–679—Average

When you are in this category, you can get fair mortgage terms and have it easy when buying smaller ticket items, (of course with no better rate than good and excellent scores). Take care not to slip down to the level where the mortgage is unaffordable. You must keep an eye on your credit report and if there are unnecessary entries, then immediately take action to fall back into your previous range.

There are many people at this level. They miss out owing to bad entries, and most of them will remain in that range.

580–619—Poor

When you are at this level, you only get credit on lenders' terms. You will probably pay more to access credit, so be ready to pay more. Also, you should remember that you cannot access auto financing if your score goes lower than this range, so you should work towards building it. This is where a large majority lie. Their score will be bad mostly owing to wrong entries. If you lie here then you will have a tough time getting credit for your budget limits and will have to be ready to pay up a lot of money.

500–579—Bad

If your credit score is in this range, access to credit will be quite high. Actually, if you are looking for a 30-year mortgage, you could be looking at 3% higher interest rates, at least, than what you would pay if you had good credit. On the other hand, if you are looking for something short time like a 36-month auto loan, you might probably pay almost double the interest rate you would pay if you had a good credit score. So being here is probably the worst thing that can happen to your credit report. You cannot possibly be here and hope to get away with low-interest rates. That is next to impossible.

Less Than 500

If your credit score goes to this level, it is so bad that it might be almost impossible to get any type of financing. If you do, the interest rates will simply be unfathomable. You might have to spend 30–40 years trying to repay it. Your entire life will be dedicated to repaying a loan and you might only get free by the time you are 50.

I am sure several of you are in this last range. But don't panic, as help is at hand. You might wonder if it is possible for you to fix your score if you are in this category and the answer is, yes! It is possible for you to improve your credit score and possibly enter the good range.

Understand that no one wants to have his or her credit score bad for the simple reason that access to credit will be too costly. It will be the worst type of score for any person to have, regardless of their borrowing habits. That's why it is paramount to take action when you start seeing inaccurate and unjustifiable entries in your report. If you spot errors that are causing you to be in this range, then you must spring into action at the earliest. To help you understand what's at stake here, let me explain to you what is at stake and why you should start following up on everything reported on your credit report, otherwise, you might end up paying more for credit than what you ought to—you don't have to learn the hard way.

To start with, I will explain a few facts about the credit reports just to put you on high alert on matters related to your credit.

A large proportion of credit reports have erroneous, unverifiable, and incorrect entries, and to be precise, 93% of credit reports have been found to have incorrect entries that affected the credit scores negatively. So, do you know what that means? It means that you and I could be having entries in our credit reports that we know nothing about; actually, we might simply discover that our credit score is ruined when our loan application is turned down. You need to look for these entries after gaining a free copy of your credit report. Now, as you have seen above on what each range of credit score means, by the time you get to the point of being turned down for a loan, your credit score is pretty much bad! You might start falling in the below 500 range and it will simply mean doom. The tiny details you see on your credit score that you don't understand where they came from could be the ones ruining your credit score. What happens is that lenders will often make some minor changes when reporting data to the CRAs—some of which taint the credit consumer's financial reputation. For instance, a change in the date of the last activity on your credit report should be something you should start worrying about. When you have something derogatory appearing in the recent activity items, your credit score will be tainted. This might be completely imaginary or simple manipulation of the actual items and entries in your report. You could even have noticed different creditors reporting the same debt multiple times, in which case your credit report will show that you are really sinking in debt even if this is not actually true. These might be some extra-large values, which will only make your score appear bad. You might also have noted the same creditor reporting the same debt in your credit report under various account numbers; this has the same effect as having multiple creditors reporting on the same debt.

Obviously, creditors could defend themselves as not knowing that these mistakes existed. However, they really care less about that, because the worse their credit score is, the more lenders charge them for credits. As was said before, they will stoop low just to get you on the hook. They will not care about your side of the story and stick to what they think is their right. So you need to be alert all throughout and do what is right for you.

The law requires that creditors can only keep information about your credit history for just 7 years. However, it isn't uncommon for lenders to keep this information for more than 10 years, which means such items will probably continue showing on your credit report year in year out, which in turn messes your credit score, and then the lenders raise the interest rates you pay. They will not be accountable to anyone and will claim to have erased any information in regard to your credit score. But they will keep using the date to bombard you by targeting specific emails and offers.

The answer to these inaccuracies in credit reports lies not in sitting around and expecting your creditors to have mercy on you because they won't. This is the problem that most people suffer from. They will think the creditor will empathize with them and help them reduce their bad credit. But they will, in fact, be interested in ruining your credit score further so that they have a chance to pull more money from you. So, the best idea is to start doing something to better your score and not waste any more time.

In any case, why do these corporations (lenders) want you to pay them for something you shouldn't pay? You must understand how these companies will try and trick you and remain alert. If at any time you find out you are being cheated owing to mistakes and errors in your credit report, you need to spring into action and deal with them at the earliest. But, what must you do to repair your credit as soon as possible?

The credit repair process can be complicated and frustrating, especially if you don't know what to do. You might get lost easily and not have a clear direction. Actually, trying to dispute on your own, without first understanding how to go about it, could probably ruin your chances of ever succeeding; that's why most people probably give up on their trial because they never did their research well. You might ruin something that can be fixed easily and also worsen your credit score in the process. So it is better to exercise precaution and try and do all the right things.

Knowing you have the right to dispute and actually disputing successfully are two totally different things, but I will teach you what to do throughout the process if you are to emerge successful in the dispute process. The key to getting derogatory items in your credit report deleted permanently is understanding and following the tested and tried credit repair processes, otherwise, you might simply start going in circles where you get an item removed and later restored in the credit report within 60 days.

Chapter 3: How to Remove Mistakes from Credit Report

Initiate a Dispute

You may initiate a dispute about an inaccurate or incomplete item on your credit report online, by telephone, or by email.

We are initiating a dare online. The three national CRAs enable you to dispute information in your credit report online. This is the simplest way.

You are initiating a dare by email. If you prefer not to utilize the internet procedure, you can email in your dispute when you have compiled a listing, and you can also prepare a letter identifying the reasons that support your dispute and every correction.

If there are mistakes—information that is outdated—or information in your credit file, you might dispute these things.

Send your correspondence for disputing the data provided and keep a copy for your records, and copies of any documents you have that support your claim. It may be helpful to add a copy of your credit report using the items. Maintain your documents.

We are initiating a dare by telephone. Call "report" to begin a dispute by telephone. (See below for directions about the best way best to locate the telephone numbers for your CRAs.)

Contact Info for the CRAs

To find contact info for initiating a credit dispute goes online. Here is where to search:

- **Equifax:** Proceed to Equifax.com. Click "Dispute something in my Equifax credit report."

- **Experian:** Proceed to Experian.com. Click on **Disputes** and on **How to Dispute** to find out how you can submit your dispute online, by email, or by telephone.

- **Transunion:** Proceed to TransUnion.com. Click on **Find out how to dispute an item in your credit report.** This page will provide you information on how you can initiate a credit dispute. (Visit the "Credit Disputes FAQs" link to find out how to submit your dispute online, by email, or by telephone.)

What Happens After You Submit Your Dispute

When the CRA receives them, it has to delete them within 3 business days after getting your dispute or reinvestigate.

When the CRA doesn't delete the data in 3 business days, it needs to

- Complete its evaluation within 45 days if you contested the data after getting your free yearly credit report (otherwise it merely contains 30 days, which is extended up to 45 days if you send the bureau additional pertinent information through the 30-day interval). In 5 business days of getting your dispute, contact the lender and report the info which you dispute
- Review and consider all pertinent information you submit and forward this info to the lender that supplied the data, and when any modifications had been made they offer you the outcomes of its reinvestigation in five business days of conclusion.

Frivolous Disputes: In many situations, the CRA has a responsibility to explore a financial product as soon as you dispute it. This implies that in case you dispute everything or nearly everything from the report—concerning that what you think is true or wrong—or you ask for reinvestigation, as the CRA might not need to research your dispute in any way.

When the CRA Does Not Respond to Your Dispute

If the CRA doesn't respond to your dispute within time constraints imposed by legislation, you might:

- **Dispute It:** You should publish the dispute and make sure you offer some new details. It may determine that your dispute is frivolous, without providing any info to the CRA, as you are not providing any information to the CRA.
- **Submit a Criticism to the CFPB:** You could also submit a complaint to the Consumer Financial Protection Bureau (CFPB). This principal agency manages CRAs, together with a copy of the disputed info you've sent to the CRA.
- **Talk with a Lawyer:** If you have exhausted the other alternatives for fixing your credit file along with the CRA and it still doesn't resolve the error or mistakes, think about talking to a

consumer law attorney who will help you enforce your rights.

- **Keep Monitoring Your Account and Credit Reports:** In some instances, you can fix the mistakes only when you aren't damaging your credit score or when you will be scheduled to fall off your credit report shortly. You ought to keep reviewing your credit reports if the mistakes are serious.

If the credit reporting agency is struggling to alter your report and you think the information is incomplete or wrong, you will want to take action. Below are a few suggestions that will assist you with your attempts:

Contact the Creditor Directly

Contact the lender who supplied the advice and demand them to inform the CRA to eliminate the information. You cannot use inaccurate information. If you receive a letter from the lender, it ought to be deleted from the credit history, and you should send a copy of the letter to the CRA that made the faulty report.

If you contact the CRA, it does not have to manage this dispute unless you supply the info. But since you think you also demonstrate a foundation for the belief, and the dispute wasn't properly researched, you should increase your complaint, because like the president or CEO, the provider is very likely to reply.

If the company cannot or won't help you in removing the info that is inaccurate, call the credit reporting agency. Credit reporting agencies have people to manage consumer disputes regarding items in their credit files, which are not eliminated through the standard reinvestigation procedure. (Visit the Equifax, Experian, and TransUnion sites to locate contact info for all these three national CRAs.)

Document another Dispute with the Credit Reporting Agency with More Information

If you have info to back up your claim, it is possible to submit a fresh dispute. Make sure to provide info. Should you dispute the mistake without giving any info to the bureau, it will determine that your dispute is frivolous, so the bureau does not need to inquire into the issue.

File a Complaint about the Credit Reporting Agency

You can file a complaint regarding a CRA as well as the Consumer Financial Protection Bureau (CFPB). The CFPB will attempt to have a response and will forward your complaint. In the event the CFPB believes that another government agency will be able to assist you, it allows you to know if they will forward your complaint.

File a Complaint Concerning the Creditor

If the lender supplied the erroneous or incomplete data fails to revise it or notify the credit reporting service of a correction (or even if it advises the CRA of this alteration but reports the incorrect information again after), you might file a complaint with the Federal Trade Commission (FTC). On the other hand, if the lender is a big institution, you might need help to file a complaint. The CFPB manages Types of agencies, and that means a complaint can document. If you are not sure which agency to contact, begin with CFPB or even the FTC, which will forward your complaint. Normally, you won't be represented by these government agencies. However, they could send an inquiry, and they may take action when there are complaints or proof of wrongdoing.

Complain about the Help of Your State Consumer Protection Agency

File a complaint with the attorney general or consumer protection bureau of your state.

Get Your Congressional Representative or Senator

After all, they write the legislation. When there are issues with all the legislation or its enforcement and you need to know, your congressperson may telephone the FTC or CFPB and request it to investigate those issues.

Consider Suing that the Credit Reporting Agency or Creditor

In the event that you were hurt after you asked for corrections, contemplate filing a lawsuit against the credit reporting bureau, as it provided inaccurate or incomplete information.

Under the Fair Credit Reporting Act (FCRA) (15 U.S.C. § 1681 and after), you might sue a CRA for negligence or deliberate non-compliance with the legislation over 2 years once you detect the damaging behavior or over 5 years after the problem took place, whichever is earlier.

Based upon the breach, you may have the ability to win punitive damages, statutory damages, damages, court costs, and attorneys' fees. You may also consider using the incorrect information that was provided.

However, these types of cases are complex and the FCRA provides tactics to creditors to prevent liability. If you would like to pursue this kind of lawsuit, you will have to speak with an attorney.

Consider Adding an Explanatory Statement for Your Credit Report

You've got the right statement for your credit score. As soon as you submit a statement regarding the dispute using a credit reporting agency, the agency must include your statement—or a list of it. It might limit your announcement if the CRA helps you write the statement. There is not a term limit. Nonetheless, it is a fantastic idea to maintain the announcement shortly. In this way, the credit reporting agency is inclined to utilize your remark.

Talk to a Lawyer

In case you need help repairing your credit report, think about talking to a consumer protection lawyer. A lawyer can help you enforce your rights from a lender or an agency that violates the FCRA.

Chapter 4: Credit Score

The Fico Scoring Model

FICO holds the distinction of most reliable credit scoring models, thanks in no small part to its longstanding track record. Fair Isaac Company began computing these scores back in 1989. They have since revised the algorithms a number of times in the past three decades to adjust for shifting factors so that they produce continuously dependable credit scores.

As we noted earlier, the traditional FICO score model will produce a score for you from 300 to 850. Scores of less than 600 equate to poor. If your score is higher than 740, then this is deemed to be excellent.

The ranges in between 600–740 mean from average to above-average creditworthiness.

In 2014, FICO introduced its FICO 9 scoring model. The primary revision in this model was to reduce the importance of unpaid medical bills. The reasoning behind this is that medical debts that are not paid are not truly financial health indicators.

You might be waiting for insurance to pay a medical bill or simply be unaware that a medical bill had been given over to a collection agency. For some people, this important change allowed their credit score to increase by up to 25 points.

Other changes in 2017 stopped collectors from reporting late medical debts that were not yet 180 days delinquent. In 2017, the three CRAs drop all of their data on civil judgments and the tax lien records from their files. FICO reported that this helped the scores of around 6% of consumers.

Before FICO 9 came out, FICO 8 (the one the company developed in 2009) was the standard credit-score version. FICO 8 remains the most commonly utilized score of the lending industry. FICO 8's distinguishing features were to penalize you for charging near your total credit limit each month and to provide clemency if you had only a single late payment of over 30 days.

It is worth noting that each time FICO releases an updated version on its scoring models, lenders may keep the version they are using or upgrade it. FICO 8 has remained the overwhelming favorite simply because it costs so much to upgrade to the new model. There are lenders still using even FICO 5 models.

You can ask your lender which model they are using when you go through the application process.

FICO scores typically do not change that much over the short term. The exception is if you start missing payments or showing charge-offs and defaults. Not everyone has a FICO score either. If you do not have credit, you will fall into the category of what experts call "credit invisible."

You must have six months of payments reported to the CRAs in order to have a FICO score.

How Is My Fico Score Calculated?

These are payment history, credit utilization, credit history, credit types, and new credit. Some categories also have sub-categories within them. We will go through each of these components next.

Payment History

Your payment history comprises 35% of your score, making it the most important single component in determining your credit score. By making your monthly payments in a timely fashion each month and not showing bad public records of lawsuits, foreclosure, or bankruptcy, you will score well here. Late payments detract from your score.

Your score is more heavily penalized the latter your payment is (2 months penalizes worse than 1 month).

Credit Utilization

The second most important category with FICO scores is your credit utilization, amounting to 30% of your total score. The key here is to stay far away from using your entire credit limit, regardless of whether you will pay the full bill when it arrives. FICO wants to see you with 30% or less of your available credit used.

This means that you should not spend over $150 each month on a $500 credit card limit.

Credit History

The next most important factor is credit history for 15% of your total score. By this, FICO means the amount of time you have possessed your credit cards. The greater amount of time you have had your first one and the longer your average credit account history, the higher your score in this category will be.

Credit Types

Your credit mix amounts to 10%. FICO is interested in the different types of credit that you possess (including credit cards, mortgages, car loans, utilities, store accounts) and the way that you pay them on time. It will help you have a better score if you count a range of different loans and credit cards on your report.

The key is not to over-apply for these accounts in a short time frame. CRAs interpret this as a warning sign that you could be desperate to get more credit.

New Credit

New credit is the final category with FICO, and it equates to 10% of their calculation. The more cards you apply for at once, the worse your score in this category will be. They see it as a possibility of you attempting to juggle your debt using new credit cards—a definite negative.

It is better for your score to spread out your applications as much as possible.

How Do You Check Your Credit Score

It's a common misconception that you will automatically get your credit score when you get a copy of your credit report. This is not entirely the case. Credit reports usually do not include your credit score. It's also important to note that you do not have only one credit score. You will have at least 3 and more if you include the Vantage score. They should be similar in range but will not usually be the same number because they are an estimate based on a series of calculations.

There are a few different ways you can try to access your credit scores. Look to our list for suggestions:

1. Check with your financial institutions. Many loaners such as credit card companies show your credit score as part of your account for free. If your creditors do not offer this, then you might be able to find the information online. Wells Fargo, for example, updates your credit score online once a month and shows how the number has changed, and what is most influencing the score. It's as easy as logging in to your account and browsing the offered resources.
2. Just like you can order credit reports, you can also order a copy of your score from the three main CRAs, and FICO directly. This is a good option if your banking institution does not offer information or you are doing your yearly credit report check.
3. Some people choose to use credit score services, or free credit monitoring services to keep track of their credit scores. Others offer greater resources and protection that charge, but there are many free ones. These are good options for those who are looking to keep track of their credit but don't want to spend the extra money for monitoring or to order directly from FICO.

What Is a FICO Score?

The credit score structure was formulated by the Fair Isaac Corporation also referred to as FICO. This credit score is utilized by financial institutions. There are other credit score models; however, the FICO score is the one that is most commonly used. Consumers can get and keep high credit scores by simply making sure their debt level remains low, and they maintain an extended history of paying their bills when they are due.

In the FICO scoring formula, not all credit reports are scored equally.

Credit scores are weighted based on the particular "scorecard" that a person falls under.

For example, if the person has filed for bankruptcy, they may be scored using a special "bankruptcy" scorecard.

The credit score for a person under one scorecard may be affected differently by negative events, like a late payment, or someone with the same event on a different scorecard.

The scorecard you're on is determined by the most recent and significant events in your credit history.

The first 10 scorecards go something like this:

Scorecards 1–5:

- Those with public records, including judgments and bankruptcy, on their credit report
- For those with serious delinquencies other than bankruptcies (60, 90, 120 latest, collections, judgments, charge-offs, repossessions, etc.)
- Those with only 1 credit account (very thin files)
- Those with only 2 credit accounts (thin files)
- Those with 3 credit accounts only

Scorecards 6–10 should NOT have ANY grave felonies (the definition of "serious" is unknown)

6. 0–2 year's oldest account

7. 2-5 year's oldest account

8. 5-12 year's oldest account

9. 12-19 year's oldest account

10. 19+ years oldest account

There is a total of 12 scorecards, and they are subject to change as FICO (formerly Fair Isaac Corp) updates its scoring formula.

What Is a Good Credit Score? How Can I Improve My Credit Rating and Credit Score?

Your credit score is split into several levels but generally ranges from 300 to 850. The different credit rating levels are labeled as follows:

- **300–600:** Bad credit
- **600–649:** Poor credit
- **650–699:** Fair credit
- **700–749:** Good credit
- **750–850:** Excellent credit

The higher your credit score, the better. Better scores allow you to get credit easier, and with lower interest rates. Even when not getting credit, such as when you are renting an apartment, having a better credit rating builds trust with potential landlords.

The best thing you can do to get your credit score up is do payments on time. As soon as you start missing payments, your score will plummet. Delinquency can turn into a negative item that is much harder to remove. If you do miss payments, communicating and maintaining a good relationship with your creditor is key.

Chapter 5: The CRAs: General Notions

CRAs are privately held, billion-dollar organizations whose primary reason for existing is to make cash; that is what revenue-driven organizations do, right? They keep data that lenders furnish them—regardless of whether accurate or inaccurate—about our credit association with them and sell it. This straightforward plan of action generates over $4 billion per year! One wellspring of income for them originates from selling the information on our credit reports to different lenders, managers, insurance agencies, credit card organizations—and whoever else you approve to see your credit information. In addition to the fact that they provide them with crude data, they likewise sell them various methods for examining the data to decide the risk of granting credit to us. In addition to trading our information to lenders, they likewise sell our information to us— credit scores, credit observing administrations, extortion security, wholesale fraud prevention. Interestingly enough, this region has quickly gotten perhaps the greatest wellspring of income. Furthermore, those are endorsed offers drop in our email inbox each week—or in our garbage email. That's right; they got our information from the CRAs as well. Organizations buy into assistance provided by the three CRAs that sell them a rundown of consumers' credit information that fits a pre-decided criterion.

Presently, as opposed to prevalent thinking, CRAs don't have any contribution on whether you ought to be endorsed a loan or not; that is absolutely based on the credit criteria of the lender you're working with. However, by utilizing the entirety of the information that has been set on your credit report (personal information, payment history, and credit propensities) and FICO's technique for scoring that data, they do tell them how creditworthy you are.

Origin and History of CRAs

In recent decades, credit has gotten easier and easier to obtain. Credit cards, for example, were once given to the wealthier classes in the public eye and were utilized just occasionally. Toward the start of the twenty-first century, practically 50% of all Americans had, in any event, one broadly useful credit card (that is, a Visa, MasterCard, American Express, or Discover card). The ascent of credit as a typical method to buy necessities, extravagances, and everything in-between implies that CRAs process more information and are a more crucial part of the general economy than any other time in recent memory. CRAs likewise monitor and investigate the data gathered from a regularly expanding number of loans for homes, cars, and other high-cost things.

Today, CRAs consistently accumulate information from creditors (banks; credit-card guarantors; mortgage organizations, which have practical experience in loaning cash to home buyers, and different institutions that give credits to people and businesses). In addition to the data gathered from creditors, credit files may likewise contain one's business history, previous addresses, false names, bankruptcy filings, and removals. Information usually remains on a credit report for 7 years before being reset.

The greater part of the nearby and provincial consumed CRAs in the United States is claimed by or are under agreement to one of the three essential consumer credit-reporting administrations referenced previously. Every one of these three organizations assembles appropriated information separately, and credit scores and reports vary somewhat from bureau to bureau. Each organization keeps up around 200 million singular consumer credit files. Frequently a lender will utilize an average of the credit evaluations provided by the three unique bureaus when choosing whether to make a loan.

Besides the 4 CRAs mentioned earlier on, another important CRA is Dun & Bradstreet (officially confirmed as the fourth designated Credit Reference Agency by the British government)". Dun & Bradstreet is the basic business credit bureau in the US as it has credit files on more than 23 million associations in North America and on more than 100 million businesses around the globe. In addition to giving creditors information important to decide a credit applicant's capabilities, CRAs make their data accessible for progressively questionable purposes. For example, standard mail advertisers regularly buy information from CRAs as they continued looking for potential clients. If you have ever gotten a letter revealing to you that you have been pre-endorsed for a particular credit card at a particular yearly percentage rate, it is valid; the credit card organization definitely realizes your credit rating and has to be sure whether to assign you the credit card or not. Forthcoming managers and proprietors sometimes buy credit histories as well.

What Do CRAs Do?

CRAs collect information from various sources in accordance with consumer information. The activity is done for various reasons and includes data from singular consumers, like the information concerning people, charge payments, and what they're getting.

Utilized for evaluating creditworthiness, the information provides lenders with an outline of your accounts if a loan repayment is required. The interest rates charged on a loan are additionally worked out concerning the kind of credit score shown by your credit report. It is, thus, not a uniform procedure, and your credit report is the significant instrument that affects future loans.

Based on risk-based valuing, it pegs various risks on various customers so as to decide the cost you will acquire as a borrower. It is done as a credit rating and is provided as assistance to various interested parties in the public. Terrible credit histories are affected, for the most part, by settled court commitments that mark you for high-interest rates every year. Duty liens and bankruptcies, for example, shut you out of the conventional credit lines and may require a great deal of arrangement for any loan to be offered by the bank.

Bureaus collect and examine credit information including financial data, personal information, and elective data. The information is from various sources, but generally from marked data furnishers. These have an exceptional association with the CRAs. An average gathering of data furnishers would be comprised of creditors, lenders, utilities, and debt collection agencies. Any association that has had payment involvement from the consumer is qualified—including courts. Any data collected for this situation is provided to the CRAs for grouping. When it is accumulated, the data is placed into specific repositories and files claimed by the bureau. The information is made accessible to customers upon request. The idea of such information is important to lenders and managers.

The information is, in this manner, material in various conditions—credit evaluation and business thought are simply part of these. The consumer may likewise require the information to check their individual score, and the home proprietor may need to check their inhabitants' report before renting an apartment. Since borrowers saturate the market, the scores will, in general, be robotic. The straightforward examination would deal with this by giving the client a calculation for speedy appraisal. Checking your score once every other year should deal with errors in your report.

Individuals from the public are qualified for one free credit report from every one of the significant bureaus. Business reports, for example, Paydex might be obtained at a request. Lawful terms for the credit bureaus incorporate consumer reporting agencies, CRAs in the US. This is organized in the Fair Credit Report Act, FCTA. Other government rules associated with the assurance of the consumer incorporate the Fair and Accurate Credit Transaction Act, Fair Credit Billing Act, and Regulation B. Statutory bodies have additionally been made for the regulation of the CRAs. The Fair Trade Commission serves as a controller for the consumer/credit reporting agencies, while the Office of the Comptroller of Currency fills in as a manager of all banks going about as furnishers.

Credit Inquiries

Next are credit inquiries. As Latoya Irby, a credit analyst, chooses to put it, a credit inquiry is a general term that covers all investigations and requests for your credit report. As you now understand, credit companies want you to have a credit report before accessing their services; as such, you are bound to create a credit report before you get real loans. But the credit companies don't just want you to set the records; they want to explore it.

Practically, this means that each time you apply for loans in a credit company, you are bound to permit them to request your credit report from a CRA. They usually do, and the detail of each inquiry is inserted in the next credit report. For example, if A/B Company had requested your report at some point, and KYC Company had also requested, JJC Company would find these companies in your credit report when you apply for another credit with them. That way they can tell the other people you have contacted how 'desperate' you have been finding some credit, and how unsuccessful you have been. That may not be an impressive opinion.

Chapter 6: Effective Strategies for Repairing Your Credit

Pay-to-Delete Strategy

If you have derogatory items in your credit report, you can opt to pay the credit balance only if the creditor agrees to delete the items from your credit report. As I already mentioned, don't agree to a $0 balance appearing on your credit report since this taints your reputation. This will ultimately improve your rating. Actually, the idea is to ensure that, whatever amount you agree to pay, it doesn't show up as your last date of the activity. If the creditor only cares about their money, why should they bother telling the world that you have finally paid?

In most instances, the creditors often write off debts within just 2 years of constant defaulting, after which this information is sold in bulk to a collection company for some pennies of a dollar. This means that the collection companies will even be just fine if you even pay a fraction of what you ought to pay. Whatever you pay, they will still make money! This makes them open to negotiations such as pay-to-delete since they have nothing to lose, anyway.

- Therefore, only use the pay-to-delete approach at this level and not at any other. Actually, the only other way around it for the collection company is a judgment, which can be costly, so you have some advantage here.

- Additionally, use this strategy when new negative items start showing up on your report that could hurt your reputation as a credit consumer.

- Also, since the creditors will often sell the same information to multiple collection companies, you might probably start noting the same debt being reported by several companies; use pay-to-delete to get them off your report.

- You can also use this strategy if you have not been successful in getting items off your credit report using other methods, as opting to go the dispute way might only make the process cyclic, cumbersome, tiresome, and frustrating; you don't want to get into this cycle.

Now that you know when to use this method, understanding how the entire process works is very critical. To start with, ensure that you get an acceptance by writing if they agree to your times; don't pay without the letter! After you agree, allow about 45 days for the next credit report to be given to you by your credit monitoring service. These companies have the legal power to initiate the deletion process, so don't accept anything less, such as updating the balance; it is either a deletion or nothing. If they try to stall the process by saying that they cannot delete the problematic item from your credit report, mention that it will only take about 5 minutes for them to fill the Universal Data Form. Don't worry if one company seems not to agree with your terms since another one will probably show up and will gladly take the offer.

In any case, what do they have to gain if they keep your debt when you are willing to pay? Remember that the records will just be in your files for 7 years, and since 2 years are already past, these companies have no choice, otherwise, you can simply let the 7 years pass! However, don't use this as an excuse for not paying your debts, since the creditors can sue you to compel you to pay outstanding amounts. The aim of this process is to ensure that whatever bad experience you have with one creditor, doesn't make the others make unfavorable decisions on your part.

Note: Don't be overly aggressive with creditors who have a lot to lose in the process, especially the recent creditors, since they can probably sue you. Your goal is to only be aggressive with creditors that are barred by the statute of limitation from suing you in court. You don't want to find yourself in legal troubles to add to your existing problems. Try and remain as smart as possible and make all the right moves to help you repair your credit at the earliest.

Pay-to-delete isn't the only option available to you; you can use other strategies to repair your credit.

Check for FDCPA (Fair Debt Collection Practices Act) Violations

The law is very clear on what collection agencies can do and what they cannot do as far as debt collection is concerned. For instance:

- They should not call you more than once a day unless they can prove that it was accidentally dialed by their automated systems.
- They cannot call you before 8.00 am or after 9.00 pm.
- They cannot threaten, belittle or yell at you to make you pay any outstanding debts.

- They cannot tell anyone else other than your spouse why they are contacting you.
- The best way to go about this is to let them know that you are recording all their calls.
- They cannot take more money from your account than you have authorized if they do an ACH.
- They are also not allowed to send you collection letters if you have already sent them a cease and desist order.

If you can prove that collection companies are in violation of the law, you should file a complaint with the company and have your lawyer send proof indicating the violations; you can then request that any outstanding debt be forgiven. You need to understand that the law is on your side in such circumstances; actually, if the violations are major, the collection companies could be forced to pay fines of up to $10,000 for these violations.

So, if your debt is significantly lower than this, you could be on your way to having your debt cleared since these companies would rather pay your debt than pay the fine. Look for errors on your credit reports.

Your credit report should be free of errors. Even the slightest thing as reporting the wrong date of last activity on your credit report is enough to damage your credit. If the write-off date is different from what has been reported, you can dispute the entry to have it corrected to reflect the actual status of your credit. However, keep in mind that the CRAs will in most instances confirm that the negative entry is correct even if this is not the case, which means that they will not remove the erroneous item.

You must put in efforts to get them on the right track. To get them to comply, you have to inform them that the law requires them to have the preponderance of their systems in place to ensure that these errors do not arise. Therefore, the mere fact of confirming the initial error is not enough; inform them about the notice (summons) and complaint to let them understand that you are serious about the matter. Once they have an idea of your stance, they will put in efforts to do the right thing. The thing is that the CRAs don't want any case to go to court since this could ultimately provide proof that their systems are weak or flawed, which means that they will probably be in some bigger problems.

So try and drive a strong point across so that they understand you mean business. The mere exchange of emails will not do, and you must send them details on how strong your case will be. This will make them understand their position, and they will decide to help you to avoid going to court. This will, in turn, work to your advantage in making them dig deeper into the issue. However, this method will only work if you are certain that an error was actually made. You will also require proof for it, so you cannot simply state that there was an error.

Request Proof of the Original Debt

If you are certain that the credit card has been written off for late payment, it is very likely that the carriers (Capital One and Citibank) cannot find the original billing statements within 30 days, which they are required by the law to respond to. This in effect allows you to have whatever entry you have disputed removed from the credit report as if it never happened.

Another handy approach is to request for the original contract that you signed to be provided to prove that you actually opened that particular credit card in the first instance. As you do this, don't just ask for "verification," since this just prompts the collection agency to "verify" that they actually received a request for collection on an account that has your name on it. Pay the original creditor.

When your debt is sold to collection agencies, you will probably risk having new items showing up on your credit report, which can further hurt your credit rating. However, you can stop that by sending a check with the full payment of any outstanding amount to the original creditor, after which you just send a proof of payment to that collection agency and any other then request them to delete any derogatory items they have reported from your credit report.

It is always a good idea to be in direct contact with your creditor or creditors. In fact, many of these agencies will be fully equipped to cheat you and will follow through on plans to have your report show bad credit scores. It is up to you to try and remove these "middlemen" and do the payment yourself. You could also enter into an agreement to pay a portion of the money to the creditor as full payment for the sum (the pay to delete strategy).

Under federal law, if the original creditor accepts any payment as full payment for any outstanding debt, the collection agency has to remove whatever they have reported. This will only work if the original creditor accepts the payment; it is possible for some of the checks you pay to the original creditor to be returned to you.

Chapter 7: What Is Credit Counselling?

At times, an individual might be faced with critical financial instability, especially when his debts are out of control. Faced with such a menace, it is advisable to take time and think of the right solution to the situation. One can even seek advice in order to reach a decision that will be too costly for oneself. The possible remedies in the market include visiting credit counselors and debt-consolidators. Both methods are common in that they will help you contain the situation. Nevertheless, you need to weigh both options to ensure that you choose the right one depending on the weight of your financial situation.

Credit counselors are professionals who will assist you to untangle your financial woes on daily basis. Individuals running these counseling firms have deep knowledge in debt management and other options that can be applied to minimize debts. Credit counselors provide several alternatives, after which the borrower can manage their debts afterwards.

With the help of the experts, the borrower prepares a realistic budget. This budget stresses mainly how the borrower spends their money. By the time the counseling process is over, the borrower will come to terms with what exactly caused the debt. The credit counselors will help the borrower to diagnose the cause so that they will not repeat the same mistake once again. The budget created eliminates any unnecessary expenditure as well as setting a tough look at the spending habits of the borrower.

The Credit counselors afterwards supply the borrower with possible options to eliminate all the financial obligations facing them. Some of the possible options are learning on debt management, debt consolidation, personal bankruptcy, and enlightenment on how to settle one's debt. Basically, the choice of these options will be catalyzed by the severity of the debt.

Generally, credit counselors will only enlighten a borrower on how to contain any debt menace on their own. These methods are effective when one is not faced with fatal punishments such as losing possession of their assets. In such situations, it is advisable to visit debt-consolidators.

Debt consolidators are somewhat similar to credit counselors in that they help borrowers contain debt menace, but debt consolidators, specifically, save borrowers from losing their property or from heading bankrupt. Plans given by debt-consolidator will give a borrower financial freedom within a short period.

Debt consolidators will require the borrower to have a good credit rating in order to qualify for their plans. If one qualifies for the consolidation plans, Debt consolidators will extend consolidation loans to them. Basically, these are loans include all the current balances the borrower has not been able to meet. The consolidation of loans relieves the borrower from any current debt obligation, so it is good for someone close to losing their assets to a lender.

For a borrower to make the right choice, they need to weigh up the benefits and limitations of each option. For example, debt management might affect future reputation, as lenders might be reluctant to give the grant a loan, as they might think the borrower is irresponsible; debt settlement might not be effective in clearing the whole portion of the loan amount, hence impairing the borrower's credit rating while the price of debt consolidation is an increased debt for settlement of the current debt.

When Is It Time to Seek Counseling

So how exactly do you know when it's time to seek out help? Well, essentially there are 3 stages of recovery that you should think about. Stage 1 is self-help. Your credit card and other debts are in such a way that you can essentially take care of it yourself through using credit elimination tactics and making small, logical decisions on how to save money and pay off debts.

Stage 2 is when your debts become unmanageable and you decide you need outside help; that's where credit counseling agencies come into play. Stage 3 is when even your outside help doesn't know what to do, and your only logical recourse is to file for bankruptcy.

It is probably time to go to credit counseling if you can't control your debt. If you can't make your payments or you know you can't pay off your debt without help, you need this type of counseling. Don't be afraid to answer your phone because it may be a collector's calling. Don't struggle to pay all your bills. Don't accept that you will be in debt for the rest of your life. Go to credit counseling.

Going to this type of counseling is better than living in fear, in debt, or filing for bankruptcy. Credit counselors may be able to negotiate with credit card companies and get interest lowered or late fees are forgiven. It is not guaranteed, but you can certainly try to find a counselor that can do so. A credit counselor will also help you figure out a budget after they look at how much you make, how much your debt is, and how much your utility bills are. Following a counselor's advice and sticking to a budget is really important when trying to get out of debt. It may be difficult, but you will have an amazing feeling when you have no more debt.

Credit counselors are not there to judge you, it is their job to help you. Get counseling recommendations from your bank, credit card companies, or a friend. Make sure a credit counselor is certified. You want a professional that knows exactly what they are doing.

Seeking credit counseling is a huge step to recovering from debt. It is the right thing to do if you have gotten in way over your head. Living in debt is not fun, and credit counseling can help you.

That being said, if your debt is actually manageable then you could just be wasting a lot of money by hiring a debt settlement or debt counseling company. In the long run, it could save you a lot of money.

Home Equity Line of Credit (HELOC)

Using a Home Equity Loan (HEL) to pay off your revolving debts will improve your credit scores, and for the same reason using any other installment loan to pay off your revolving debt will work.

FICO gives less weight to installment loan debt.

You just need to make sure you use a Home Equity LOAN and not a Home Equity Line of Credit (HELOC).

A HELOC is scored just like a credit card by FICO, so using it wouldn't improve your scores.

Just be sure to use it to pay down your debt and not as a way to get yourself into more debt.

If you're not disciplined enough to run up your balances again, then this would not be a smart move for you.

I include it because it works, but you have to pick and choose what works for YOU.

Credit Builder Loans

Some lenders offer a secured loan program designed to help you rebuild your credit. They're called credit builder loans.

Although it is a slow process, it is a very effective method for boosting your scores. It's slower because it's an installment loan. Installment loans have less of an impact on your credit score.

Be that as it may, in over 6–12 months, you will see your credit score increase. That's because you need a few installment loans to improve the "Credit Mix" which is responsible for 10% of your credit score.

Here's how your scores are determined:

FICO SCORES IMAGE

The Ideal Ratio Is:

- 2–4 credit cards
- A car loan, home loan, and personal loan
- 1–2 retail cards

The credit builder loan completes the personal loan portion of the equation.

Here's How It Works:

- The amount you borrow is deposited into an escrow account.
- You can't touch it until the loan is paid.
- You make your regular payments each month, building your credit score as you go.
- When you're done paying, you get the full balance plus interest, and you can do with it as you please.

The Traditional Features Include:

- Loan amounts from $500–$3000
- 12–24 month terms
- Loan funds earn dividends
- Loan interest rate fixed at 5%

So, for example, a $1000 loan at 5% over 18 months would equal payments of $57.79.

The terms may change from bank to bank, so you need to shop around.

Rating Agencies

Who Are the Rating Agencies?

Contrary to what the term "agency" might suggest, these are private for-profit organizations and not regulatory or government organizations.

The rating agencies' business model is based primarily on remuneration paid by rated entities, advisory activities, and the dissemination of rating data.

Rating Agencies and the Financial Crisis

Rating agencies are accused of participating in the outbreak of the 2007–2009 financial crisis for two reasons. First of all, they tended to note too much complacently titles that eventually turned out to be "toxic," despite (or because of?) the sophisticated financial packages on which they rest. When real estate market conditions began to deteriorate in the United States, they reacted by sharply lowering the rating of many assets ("downgrading"), contributing to the downward spiral in which the market was driven.

The agencies had already aroused criticism during bankruptcies that they had been totally unable to anticipate (Parmalat, Enron, WorldCom, etc. Subsequently). They were again singled out during the Greek debt crisis.

Chapter 8: Guaranteed Methods to Protect Credit Score

Do Not Fully Use Your Credit Cards

30% of your score is how you use your credit. For example, having a credit card with a $10,000 limit is amazing! You can do whatever you want with it, and trust me, that is something I often did. But, that is actually another thing that can gravely affect your credit score. You want to make sure you are only using up to 30% of your credit card. "But Alan, what is the point of having a $10,000 card limit if I can only use $3,000?!" Great question! Let me explain it in more detail. By the end of the billing month, you only want to have, at most, 30% on your credit card balance. You can use the full amount of the credit card if you want, just pay it off before the end of the billing month. A simple and fun example goes like this: if I wanted to be a baller and buy 500 large pizzas for a block party, at the cost of $15 each (and I was in some weird loophole where taxes were exempt). I would have placed $7,500 on my credit card, even though I already had $2,000 on my card. That is clearly 95% of my card limit! But, if I turned around and paid everything off my credit card, the end of my billing month would show that I had $2,000 debt. My credit score will not be negatively affected by buying food for the best block party in existence! Now, in a perfect world, paying off your cards in their entirety, by the end of the billing month, is by far the best thing you can do. Pay what you can but stay under 30%! Hacking Your Way to That Perfect Score

The above image is a fantastic simple guide to climbing up that credit score ladder. Now, that looks nice, but what exactly is considered "excellent" credit? Well, after searching and searching, it seems as though you are considered excellent when your credit score reaches 760. That number seems to be the number that is in the goldilocks zone in the credit score world. With an excellent credit score rating, you will have the best interest rates, you will have the least amount of issues attempting to get loans, and you will, most definitely, never have to leave a deposit whenever you want to turn on your utilities at the brand new home you will buy with that amazing mortgage rate you will get! You need to make sure you cover everything. If you have missed/late payment marks on your credit report, reach out to that credit card company and ask them to get them removed! Let them know of the reason why you were not able to pay them on time and then let them know of the good standing you are with them while letting them know of your goals of improving your credit score. I have got 3 late payment marks taken off within a month!

If you had collection marks on your credit report, and you went through the process of trying to remove them but still ended up paying, wait a few months and send them a letter asking to get them removed. This may work. But if you really want it to work, send a lot of letters, 2–3 a week until someone who gets paid $10 an hour does not want to deal with it anymore and removes the marks from the credit report. I have done it once, and though at first, I felt shameful, 3 months later I no longer had them! I must have broken through to someone! Win!

If you are new to getting credit, having a 9-year worth of credit history will definitely be a difficult task, so you may have to wait. But in that time, follow this guide and make sure you are making all your payments on time! For those of you who have been around for quite some time, do not close your credit cards. If you have to, then please be wary, but I would hold on to any and all credit cards and never close them. If you do not want to use them anymore, just don't use them.

CHAPTER 9: FCRA AND SECTION 609

What Is Section 609?

A 609 is known as a dispute letter, which you would send to your creditor if you saw you were overcharged or unfairly charged. Most people use a 609 letter in order to get the information they feel they should have received. There are several reasons why some information might be kept from you.

A section 609 letter is sent after two main steps. First, you see that the dispute is on your credit report. Second, you have already filed and processed a debt validation letter. The basis of the letter is that you will use it in order to take unfair charges off your credit report, which will then increase your credit score.

The 609 letters can easily help you delete your bad credit. Other than this, there are a couple of other benefits you will receive from the letter. One of these benefits is that you will obtain your documentation and information as the credit bureau has to release this information to you. Secondly, you will be able to obtain an accurate credit report, which can definitely help you increase your credit score.

There are also disadvantages to the 609 letters. One of these disadvantages is that collection agencies can add information to your credit history at any time. A second disadvantage is that you still have to repay debt. You cannot use the 609 letters in order to remove the debt that you are obligated to pay. Finally, your creditor can do their own investigation and add the information back into your credit report, even if it was removed (Irby, 2019).

One of the reasons section 609 came to be is because one of five people states they have inaccurate information on the credit report (Black, 2019). At the same time, many people believe that this statistic is actually higher than 20 percent of Americans.

How Section 609 Works to Repair Bad Credit

If you notice anything on your report that should not be there, you need to use the section 609 loophole in order to file a dispute, which could result in their wrong information being taken off of the report. If this is the case, your credit score will increase, as you will no longer have this negative inaccuracy affecting your score.

How to File a Dispute With Section 609

It is important to note that there are several template letters for section 609. What this means is that you can easily download and use one of these templates yourself. While you usually have to pay for them, there are some that are free. Of course, you will want to remember to include your information in the letter before you send it.

You will want to make sure everything is done correctly, as this will make it more likely that the information will come off and no one will place it back on your report again.

1. Find a dispute letter through Googling "section 609 dispute letters". While you might be able to find a free download, for some, you will be able to copy and paste into Microsoft Word or onto a Google Doc.

2. Make the necessary changes to the letter. This will include changing the name and address. You will also want to make sure your phone number is included. Sometimes people include their email address, but this is not necessary. In fact, it is always safer to only include your home address or PO Box information. You will also want to make sure to edit the whole letter. If something does not match up to what you want to say in your letter, such as what you are trying to dispute on your credit report, you need to state this. These letters are quite generic, which means you need to add in your own information.

3. You want to make sure that all of your account information you want to be taken off your credit report is handwritten. You also want to make sure you use blue ink rather than black. On top of this, you do not need to worry about being too neat, but you want to make sure they can read the letters and numbers correctly. This is an important part of filing your dispute letter because handwritten ones in blue ink will not be pushed through their automated system. They have an automatic system that will read the letter for them and punch in the account number you use. They will then send you a generic letter that states these accounts are now off your credit report, which does not mean that it actually happened. When you write the information down, a person needs to read it and will typically take care of it. Of course, this does not mean that you will not be pushed aside. Unfortunately, this can happen with any letters.

4. You want to make sure that you prove who you are with your letters. While this is never a comfortable thing to do, you must send a copy of your social security card and your driver's license or they will shred your letter. You also need to make sure that you get each of your letters notarized. You can typically do this by visiting your county's courthouse.

5. You can send as many letters as you need to; however, keep in mind that the creditor typically will not make you send more than four. This is because when you threaten to take them to court in the third letter, they will realize that your accounts and demands just are not worth it. First, you could damage their reputation, and secondly, you will cost them more money than simply taking the information off your credit report will.

6. You must make sure that you keep all correspondence they send you. This will come in handy when they try to make you send more information or keep telling you that they cannot do anything. It is important that you do not give up. Many people struggle to get them to pay attention because that is just how the system works. Therefore, you need to make sure that you do not listen to their quick automatic reply that your information is off of your credit report. You also want to make sure to wait at least three months and then re-run your credit report to make sure the wrong information has been removed. Keep track of every time you need to re-run your credit report as you can use this as proof if they continue to send you a letter stating the information is off of your credit report. It is important to note that you can now file a dispute letter online with all three credit bureaus.

However, this is a new system, which means that it does come with more problems than sending one through the mail. While it is completely your choice whether you use a form to file your 609 dispute or send a letter, you always want to make sure you keep copies and continue to track them, even if you don't hear from the credit bureau after a couple of months. It will never hurt to send them a second letter or even a third.

Why Use a 609 Letter?

The 609 Letter is going to be one of the newest credit repair secrets that will help you to remove a lot of information on your credit report, all of the false information and sometimes even the accurate information, thanks to a little loophole that is found in our credit reporting laws.

You can use this kind of letter in order to resolve some of the inaccuracies that show up, to dispute your errors, and handle some of the other items that could inaccurately come in and impact and lower your credit score.

Using these 609 letters is a good way for us to clean up our credit a bit and in some cases; it is going to make a perfect situation. However, we have to remember that outside of some of the obvious benefits that we are going to discuss, there are a few things that we need to be aware of ahead of time.

There are few limitations that are going to come with this as well, for example, even after you work with the 609 letters, it is possible that information that is seen as accurate could be added to the report again, even after the removal. This is going to happen if the creditor is able to verify the accuracy. They may take it off for a bit if the 30 days have passed and they are not able to verify at that point. But if the information is accurate, remember that it could end up back on the report.

CHAPTER 10: HOW TO WRITE A CREDIT REPAIR LETTER 609

General Advice to See Success With 609

Whether you want to delete just one thing from your record or you are looking to delete a lot of different things at the same time, you want to make sure that your 609 Letter is taken care of and ready to go. There are a lot of parts that need to go through in order to get this done, but when you look at some of the templates, you will see that this is not as bad as it may seem.

When you are ready to write out some of the letters you need to send out to the credit agencies, and you are getting all of the documentation ready to go, make sure to follow some of the general advice that we have below:

Keep all of the records

Everything has to be recorded on your end of things. Don't just send out a letter and then assume that it is going to be all good. You never know when things are going to go missing or when you will need to prove your side of things. And the more accurate and in-depth records you are able to take, the better it will be with everyone.

This means that we need to keep track of everything, from the moment that we start sending out information and letters to the credit bureaus all the way until way after the fact when they take that information off your credit report. This will help you if anything comes back later on, or you need to make sure that you can prove your side of the story if the credit agency doesn't respond or do what they are supposed to.

Keep track of everything that you can along the way. You should have all of the letters that you send out, both the originals and any follow-ups that you send as well. If the credit agency gets back in touch with you, then you should keep the letters they send to you and your responses back. You can hold onto all of the supporting documents that you send each time as well. The more information that you add to your records about this, the better it will be for getting your way in the process.

Add in the Identification Information

Before you send out any information or work with section 609, make sure that you send along with it some identification information. This is going to make sure that the credit agency is going to understand who you are and can prove that they are actually working with the person who says they own the account or at least own the SSN that goes with all that information on the credit report.

There are a lot of different options that you are able to use for showing your identity, and you should include a number of them with your letter to help prove who you are. You would want to work with information like your driver's license, social security numbers, and more to showcase who you are and why you need to make a difference in the credit report.

Consider Bringing Something Up, Even if it Doesn't Seem Important

While you are at this process, it is worth bringing up even some of the smaller things that are on your report. Even if these don't seem important at the time, and they are not the main thing that you want to put your time and attention are, while you are writing the letter, you should add in as many details and as many disputes that are legitimate as possible.

You never know what you would be able to get erased off the credit report, and how much of a difference that is going to make to your credit score along the way. Even if the item seems small, you should consider adding it to the dispute that you will do.

Sometimes, the time limit will go on too long, and the agency will not respond. If this happens, all of the items, whether they are big or small, will need to be taken out of the report. And you will find that even a few small things can add up to be big things in the long run. Even if the credit agency won't erase all of the little things, it doesn't really take much of a difference along the way in terms of the time that you take to get it all done. And it could make a difference.

Do Not Contact the FTC

One thing that a lot of people are going to try and use is to contact the FTC and other agencies in the hope of getting things fixed. They may hope that because there is something wrong with the credit report, the FTC will be able to help them take care of this. Sometimes they are mad and want to get the agency in trouble for falsely adding things to their reports. And other times, they may just not know who they are supposed to contact.

However, this is not going to do you any good. If you contact the FTC, they are not going to be able to provide you with the assistance that you need. In fact, their stance is that they are not going to get in between you and the credit agency at all, and all you will get back is a form letter stating these facts. Since you have other options at your disposal to work with, you do not need to work with the FTC, but just make sure that you are going to not waste time in the process.

When you want to get something on your credit report fixed and all better, then it is important to not waste time with the FTC, and instead go straight to the credit agencies. You can send the same letter and the same information to each one, and they are the ones who will be able to help us to get things done. If you follow the rules that we are using here, and some of the other steps that we talked about in this section, you will be able to get your credit report taken care of.

Send a Letter to Each Credit Agency

One thing that we need to remember here is that we have to go through the process of sending out one of these Section 609 letters to each credit agency that we want to get to remove the items. The credit agencies are not going to talk to one another about this. If you send out a letter to Transunion, but not to one of the others, then Transunion may take it off your report, but none of the others would do this for you.

You have to be responsible for sending a letter to all three of the reporting agencies if you would like to get that debt taken out of all of your reports. You should automatically send this information to all three right from the start, so make sure to get copies of all the information so that you are ready to go and handle all of that at once as well.

You can include the same information in each of the letters that you send out. And you can even send out the same letter, just make sure to change the company and department name that you are using on each one. Then include the same proofs of your identity, the credit reports, and more, for each one to get the ball rolling here.

Mention Section 609 in the Letter

There are a few different things that we need to remember when it comes to writing out our form letters. We need to include our name and some of the information about who we are and where we live. We need to include information about the debts and accounts that we would like to dispute along the way, including a credit report to show what accounts were talking about. And then we need to make sure that we, at some point, mention the section 609 in the letter.

This is going to be useful in several aspects. First, it is going to show the credit agency that you know what you are talking about. There are a lot of people out there who would like to fix their credit scores, but they don't understand the laws, or they are trying to sneak things past. The credit agencies are going to notice these individuals easily and will not want to work with them at all.

But when you go through and mention the Section 609 in your letter, like we have talked about so far in this guidebook, then you will find that it is much easier for you to grab their attention. You actually have done your research, you know what your rights are, and you are ready to take them on to get the credit report taken care of. The credit agencies are going to notice and respect this, and that will make it more likely that they will listen to you and send out the information that you need or erase the information that should not be there.

Mention the 30-Day Limit

In addition to making sure that you mention something about Section 609 in the letter you send out, you need to also make sure that you mention the 30 days that the agency gets to respond to you. This not only helps to show that you have a good idea about what you are talking about here but will make it easier for you to remind the credit agency about this right that you have with the Section 609 that we talk about here.

The letters that we have below will have examples of how you are able to write these out in your own form letter. But make sure to mention this and that you expect the credit agency to respond and work with that time limit in order to get things taken care of. If you do this, then it is a lot harder for them to come back with not knowing about the time limit and sets out the same expectations that everyone on both sides needs to follow.

Use One of the Templates So You Know Where to Start

Making sure that you have included all of the right parts in your letter is going to be a challenge. You want to make sure that you write it out in the right manner, that you mention the right parts about Section 609, and you want to make sure that you sound like you know what you are talking about along the way.

The good news is that we have provided some templates that we are able to use in order to take care of this process. There are several Section 609 templates that you are able to work with at the end of this guidebook, and they will be able to provide you with the right way to word your letters to get them noticed. They will mention the Section 609, the FCRA, and even the 30-day notice that is important so that you can really write out a letter that is going to get noticed and can help you to clean out your credit report.

Send a Follow-Up Letter

We may think that all of the work is done, and we won't have to do anything else after we send off the initial letter to all three credit agencies. But unfortunately, there are a few other steps that we need to complete. Once you are certain that the 30 days have passed and you have given the company enough time to respond to what you sent in, it is time to send in the follow-up a letter telling them that it is now their responsibility to remove that information from your credit report.

We are going to provide you with a good template that you can use at the end of this guidebook for the follow-up letter. But it basically will tell the agency that you sent in information about the different disputes you had on your credit report, and since they have not replied in the timely manner given by the FRCA in Section 609, it is now time for them to remove those items from your credit report.

These letters are short and sweet and will not have a lot to them. They will summarize some of the information that you sent out to them a month ago, and then reiterate what your rights are under Section 609 and what you expect the credit agency to do now that the right amount of time has passed. Depending on the length of your original dispute, this letter could be long or short.

There are a lot of misconceptions out there when it comes to working with the Section 609 letter, and getting it right is going to make the difference between whether you are able to get the credit agency to do what you would like, which would then increase your credit score, or not. Following the advice in this chapter will help to make this whole process easier as well.

What Do I Include in My Credit Dispute Letter?

When you write a letter of credit dispute to a credit bureau, you first need to locate your credit report – this may be a bigger challenge than it sounds, particularly because the credit bureau in question might have details from almost everybody in the country you are reporting. After you have found your report, you may need to include details about the mistake, as well as a clarification as to why you are contesting the object. And finally, your letter of credit dispute should include a request to the credit bureau to delete the item from your credit report.

By supplying the office with the requisite details, it should have everything it needs to make a decision on your case.

Here's what you need to add:

- The present date of entry

- Your information (name, contact information, date of birth, and account number)

- Contact information for the credit bureau

- A short explanation of the mistake (no need to make it a long and complicated story)

- Any documentation you may have that may help prove your case, such as payment records or court documents (make sure you submit them in a letter)

- Directions on what you want the credit bureau to do (re-investigate and delete the item from your report)

- Copy of your credit report with the bug highlighted

- A scanned copy of your government ID (such as your driver's license) and a bill or other document to show your address

Cease and Desist Letters

The reasons that you might want to send a cease-and-desist letter and the pros and cons of doing so were explained. You want to include your contact information and the account number that you want to stop being contacted about. Use this as a last resort for stopping collection companies as it can backfire, leading to your case being brought to court. Writing a cease-and-desist letter is quite different from writing a dispute letter. Pay attention to their differences.

To make a cease and desist letter you should:

- Use professional yet firm language.

- Reference the Fair Debt Collections Practice Act (FDCPA).

- Keep all original copies for your records.

- Send your letter via certified mail.

To make a cease and desist letter you should not:

- Incriminate yourself in anything that the collection agency might have accused you of doing.

- Use personal language.

Cease and Desist Letter Template

Date

Your Name

Your Address

Your City, State, Zip Code

Name of Collection Agency

Address

City, State, Zip Code

Re: Account Number

To [Name of Collection Agency],

Under the Fair Debt Collections Practices Act (FDCPA), Public laws 95 – 109 and 99 – 361, I am formally notifying you to cease all communications with me regarding my debt for this account and any other debts that you have purported that I owe.

I will file an objection with the Federal Trade Commission and the [Your State] Attorney General's office as well as pursue criminal and civil claims against you and your company if you attempt to continue contacting me after you receive this notice. If I receive any further communications after you have confirmed receipt of this notice, the communications may be recorded as evidence for my claims against you.

You should also be aware that any negative information related to this account on my credit reports will be handled with all legal rights available to me.

Regards,

Your Name

Signature

Goodwill Letters

Goodwill letters are not a guaranteed method of removing negative information from your credit report but are still worth a try in some situations. They are more effective if you have a good history with the company, have had a technical error delayed your payment, or if your autopay did not go through. You can sometimes even convince a credit company to forgive a late payment if you simply forgot to pay.

Try to contact your credit agency by phone to negotiate and explain your situation before sending a goodwill letter. This tactic might be all that you need to do in order to remove the record of the late payment. The sooner you contact, the better as well. If you notice that you have a late payment, calling right away could stop it from being reported at all.

To write a goodwill letter you should:

- Use courteous language that reflects your remorse for the late payment and thank the company for their service.

- Include reasons you need to have the record removed such as qualifying for a home or auto loan or insurance.

- Accept that you were at fault for the late payment.

- Explain what caused the payment to be made late.

To write a goodwill letter you should not:

- Be forceful, rude, or flippant about the situation.

Goodwill Letter Template

Date

Your Name

Your Address

Your City, State, Zip Code

Name of Credit Company

Address

City, State, Zip Code

Re: Account Number

Dear Sir or Madam,

Thank you [company's name] for continued service. I am writing in regard to an urgent request concerning a tradeline on my credit reports that I would like to have reconsidered. I have taken pride in making my payments on time and in full since I received [name of credit line/card] on [date that you received the credit]. Unfortunately, I was unable to pay on time [date of missed payment(s)] due to [detailed and personal reason for not being able to pay on time. You might want to include several sentences using as much information as possible to plead your case.]

[Follow up your reason for not paying on time with a concession of guilt such as:] I have come to see that despite [reason listed above], I should have been better prepared/more responsible with my finances to ensure the payment was on time. I have worked on [some type of learning or way of improving your situation] in order to prevent this situation from happening again.

I am in need of/about to apply for [new credit line such as a home loan] and it has come to my attention that the notation on my credit report of [credit company's] late payment may prevent me from qualifying or receiving the best interest rates. Due to the fact that this notation is not a reflection of my status with [credit company], I am requesting that you please give me another chance at a positive credit rating by revising my tradelines.

If you need any additional documentation or information from me in order to reach a positive outcome, please feel free to contact me.

Thank you again for your time,

Sincerely yours,

Your Name

Signature

Other Letter Templates

Letter #1 (Initial Letter to Credit Bureau Disputing Items)

{Name of bureau}

{Address}

{Date}

{Name on account}

{Report number}

To whom it may concern:

On {date of credit report} I received a copy of my credit report, which contains errors that are damaging to my credit score. I am requesting the following items be completely investigated as each account contains several mistakes.

{Creditor 1 / Account number}

{Creditor 2 / Account number}

{Creditor 3 / Account number}

Thank you in advance for your time. I understand that you need to check with the original creditors on these accounts and that you will make sure every detail is accurate. I also understand that under the Fair Credit Reporting Act you will need to complete your investigation within 30 days of receiving this letter. Once you are finished with your investigation, please send me a copy of my new credit report showing the changes. I look forward to hearing from you as I am actively looking for a new job and wouldn't want these mistakes on my credit report to stand in my way.

Sincerely,

{Your signature}

{Your printed name}

{Your address}

{Your phone number}

{Your social security number}

Include a copy of the credit report showing which accounts you are disputing

Letter #2 (When You Don't Get a Response From Letter #1)

{Name of bureau}

{Address}

{Date}

{Name on account}

{Report number}

To whom it may concern:

On {date of your first letter} I sent you a letter asking you to investigate several mistakes on my credit report. I've included a copy of my first letter and a copy of the report with the mistakes circled. The Fair Credit Reporting Act says I should only have to wait 30 days for the investigation to be finished. It has been more than 30 days and I still have not heard anything.

I'm guessing that since you have not responded that you were not able to verify the information on the mistaken accounts. Since it has been more than 30 days, please remove the mistakes from my credit report and send me a copy of my updated credit report. Also, as required by law, please send an updated copy of my credit report to anyone who requested a copy of my credit file in the past six months.

I look forward to hearing from you as I am actively looking for a new job and wouldn't want these mistakes on my credit report to stand in my way.

Sincerely,

{Your signature}

{Your printed name}

{Your address}

{Your phone number}

{Your social security number}

Include a copy of the credit report showing which accounts you are disputing

Include a copy of your original letter

Include a copy of the registered letter receipts showing the date they received your original letter

Letter #3 (Request for Removal of Negative Items From the Original Creditor)

{Name of creditor}

{Address}

{Date}

{Name on account}

To whom it may concern:

On {date of credit report} I received a copy of my credit report which contains errors that are damaging to my credit score. I am requesting the following items be completely investigated as each account contains several mistakes.

{Description of item(s) you are disputing/account number(s)}

I have included a copy of the credit report and have highlighted the account(s) in question.

Thank you in advance for your time. I understand that you need to check on these accounts and that you will make sure every detail is accurate. I also understand that under the Fair Credit Reporting Act you will need to complete your investigation within 30 days of receiving this letter. Once you are finished with your investigation, please alert all major credit bureaus where you have previously reported my information. Also, please send me a letter confirming the changes.

I look forward to hearing from you as I am actively looking for a new job and wouldn't want these mistakes on my credit report to stand in my way.

Sincerely,

{Your signature}

{Your printed name}

{Your address}

{Your phone number}

{Your social security number}

Include a copy of the credit report showing which accounts you are disputing

Letter #4 (If You Don't Receive a Response From Letter #3)

{Name of creditor}

{Address}

{Date}

{Name on account}

To whom it may concern:

On {date of your first letter} I sent you a letter asking you to investigate several mistakes on my credit report. I've included a copy of my first letter and a copy of the report with the mistakes circled. The Fair Credit Reporting Act says I should only have to wait 30 days for the investigation to be finished. It has been more than 30 days and I still have not heard anything.

I'm guessing that since you have not responded, you were not able to verify the information on the mistaken accounts. Since it has been more than 30 days, please immediately report the updated information to all major credit bureaus so they may update my credit report. Also, please send me a letter confirming these changes to the way you report my account.

I look forward to hearing from you as I am actively looking for a new job and wouldn't want these mistakes on my credit report to stand in my way.

Sincerely,

{Your signature}

{Your printed name}

{Your address}

{Your phone number}

{Your social security number}

Include a copy of the credit report showing which accounts you are disputing

Include a copy of your original letter

Include a copy of the registered letter receipts showing the date they received your original letter

Letter #5 (If the Credit Bureau Doesn't Remove Negative Items Disputed)

{Name of credit bureau}

{Address}

{Date}

{Name on account}

{Report number}

To whom it may concern:

On {date of your first letter} I sent you a letter asking you to investigate several mistakes on my credit report. I've included a copy of my first letter and a copy of the report with the mistakes circled. According to your response, you have chosen to leave these negative items on my credit report adding insult to injury. The items in question are:

{Creditor 1 / Account number}

{Creditor 2 / Account number}

{Creditor 3 / Account number}

I find it completely unacceptable that you and the creditor refuse to investigate my dispute properly. Your refusal to follow the Fair Credit Reporting Act is causing me untold stress and anxiety. Since you won't follow through, I want to know exactly how you investigated each account. Therefore, I would like the name, title, and contact information of the person at the creditor with whom you did the investigation. This will allow me to personally follow up with the creditor and find out why they are choosing to report these mistakes on my credit, month after month.

I know I am only one person among thousands or more that you have to look after, but to me, this is both personally damaging and humiliating. You may not understand it and you don't have to—all I'm asking is that when people look at my credit file, they see the most accurate information and that's not what's happening.

Please provide me with the requested information right away so I can finally put this nightmare behind me.

I look forward to hearing from you as I am actively looking for a new job and wouldn't want these mistakes on my credit report to stand in my way.

Sincerely,

{Your signature}

{Your printed name}

{Your address}

{Your phone number}

{Your social security number}

Include a copy of the credit report showing which accounts you are disputing

Include a copy of your original letter

Include a copy of the bureau's response showing no changes to your credit

CHAPTER 11: WHAT ARE MY RIGHTS UNDER 609?

The Fair Credit Reporting Act is going to cover many of the aspects and the components of credit checking to make sure of maintaining a reasonable amount of privacy and accuracy along the way. This agency is going to list all of the responsibilities that credit reporting companies and any credit bureaus will have, and it includes the rights of the consumer that will be your rights in this situation. This Act is going to be the part that will govern how everything is going to work to ensure that all parties are treated in a fair manner.

When using this act the consumer has to be told if any of the information that is on your file has been in the past or is now being used against you in any way, shape, or form. You have a right to know whether the information is harming you and what that information is. In addition, the consumer is going to have the right to go through and dispute any information that may be seen as inaccurate or incomplete at the time. If they see that there are items in the documents they are sent, if the billing to them is not right or there is something else off in the process, the consumer has the right to dispute this and the credit reporting agency needs to at least look into it and determine if the consumer is right.

This Act is going to limit the access that third parties can have to your file. You personally have to go through and provide your consent before someone else goes through and looks at your credit score, whether it is a potential employer or another institution providing you with funding.

They are not able to get in and just look at it. Keep in mind that if you do not agree for them to take a look at the information, it is going to likely result in you not getting the funding that you want, because there are very few ways that the institution can fairly assess the risk that you pose to them in terms of creditworthiness.

It means that you may have debt or another negative item that is on your credit report, but there is a way to get around this without having to wait for years to get that to drop off your report or having to pay back a debt that you are not able to afford.

Keep in mind that this is not meant to be a method for you to take on a lot of debts that you cannot afford and then just dump them. But on occasion, there could be a few that you are able to fight and get an instant boost to your credit score in the process.

CHAPTER 12: DEBT SNOWBALL

Credit is actually the money available to be loaned out. It is the ability of an individual to take on debts serving as a kind of backup funds to provide you with the means of getting what you need. Credit is used to make the purchase of goods and services with borrowed money. A credit card company or a bank creates a credit account for you with a maximum amount of money you can borrow, making it your credit limit. The common sources of credit are personal loans, student loans, car loans, mortgages, and credit cards. If your available credit is greater than your current level of debts, loaners will see you as creditworthy when you want to borrow. A credit card is a card useful for basic transactions where you sign on purchases, with the exemption of gas payment, and pay interest on the purchases made in 30 days. Debt, on the other hand, refers to the money that is borrowed to be paid back at a later time with a specific interest. It can also be said to be the result of borrowing money from lenders. Debt happens when you make use of your available credit. It is the actual money you owe, of which you are supposed to pay back to your creditors. To put it simply, credit is how much you can borrow while debt is the exact amount of money you owe to your creditors. A debit card is a card that allows you to make payments of purchases made by sending the payment directly from your bank account to your creditors.

Debts

Millions of people are neck-deep in debts of business loans, mortgages, personal loans, etc. It is rather difficult to stay away from debts or pay them off if there is no proper debt management. Most people find that the debts keep piling up, no thanks to the interest rates attached. They go into debt because they either spend more than they earn or lack the discipline to inculcate the habit of paying off their debt. It is in your best interest to seek out professional advice on how to manage your debts especially if you find it very difficult to repay them back. Consider speaking to your creditors too without delay so you can work out how best to repay these loans.

Why do People Acquire Debts?

1. Poor Money Management: This is a no-brainer, and probably the biggest reason people acquire debt. It obviously speaks for itself. When you don't have a proper budget or lack the discipline to track your daily and monthly spending, you'll surely move down the road to debt faster than you can think especially if you earn lower than you spend. Lack of budget invokes debt. You will not be able to curb unnecessary expenditures and you might have to take up a loan to keep up with those expenses.

2. Income: Sometimes in life, we get hit with unexpected changes like a job or income crises. There could be a problem at your workplace when workers' pay gets reduced or employees get fired.

The sudden change in income or loss of a person's livelihood is another huge factor that influences people into becoming debtors. When people find themselves with a lesser income for whatever reason, they fail to handle such a situation accordingly.

Most people cannot deal with change, certainly, the one negatively attached to their occupation. Failure to tailor your expenses in line with your low income thereby letting your expenses exceed the said income pushes you to take up loans after loans that you definitely will not be able to pay off. Not in record time at least. The key thing here is a proper budget.

3. Gambling: Here is another huge reason people go into debt. Due to its entertaining and addictive nature, those who gamble are stuck with it helplessly. Gamblers cannot seem to drop the foul habit. Sometimes, all it takes is just one try and they get hooked forever, gambling all their life away only to later turn up in the streets homeless. When the debts keep piling up without a way out, with unbearable pressure from creditors/loan sharks, most gamblers are driven to crime.

Lenders play on gamblers' addiction, always offering to give out more loans even when the previous debts have not been paid off until such gambler gets in so deep that whatever he owns gets transferred to his creditor. Gambling, however, is a game and a business, a dangerous one at that albeit entertaining as well as lucrative.

4. Lack of Savings: Not saving up for the "rainy day" is yet another reason people go into debt. When you have nothing put aside for future expenditure, expected or unexpected, relating to severe health issues, unemployment, death of a family member, etc., you will have no choice but to seek out lenders. Having nothing saved can never bring you anything good but a burden like debt.

5. Medical Expenses: It is the 21st century where doctors and hospitals are charging much more over medical treatments. One can hardly blame them though. Those treatments are costly to make, and the world is advancing more. While the high cost of treatments especially for severe health cases cannot be blamed on hospitals, their growing impatience at people who are unable to pay up their medical bills on time is appalling. It is another reason people get swamped in the very deep ocean of debts. Taking out a loan or pulling your medical expenses on your credit cards becomes so much easier when you do not have the money to pay for your bills.

6. Divorce: American laws rule over what should be done with a couple's money during a divorce settlement, which, by the way, is another way a person can acquire so many debts. Should a party demand way too much during the divorce

proceedings, the other party has no choice but to go whatever length to meet up with his/her partner's demands, else he faces a jail term or a court fine. Not to mention paying off attorneys to represent his/her case. Divorce is seen by some as a gold mining.

Types of Debts

- **Protected debt**: This is defined by the need for collateral. It provides security to the moneylender that the borrower will pay up else risk losing the collateral placed on the line. The collateral can be a house, a car, or any other valuable property.

- **Unsecured debt**: Here, the creditor's security is based on a high-interest rate that the debtor has to pay for along the principal loan amount. There is no collateral like credit cards nor personal loans.

- **Fixed payment debt**: An example of this is a mortgage which has the same interest rate for the complete timeline of the loan. Mortgages are loans made to purchase homes with the subject real estate serving as collateral on the loan.

- **Variable interest rate debt**: The interest rate in this circumstance can vary over the existence of the loan just like credit cards.

- **Fixed payment term**: Here, the loan is set to be paid by an already fixed date like student loans or mortgages.

- **Variable repayment period**: This type of debt has no fixed date when the debt must be paid like a credit card.

- **Deductible**: This type of loan is used to make personal conditions better and by effect have tax benefits just like in mortgages or student loans.

- **Nondeductible**: This is a loan that is not used in purchasing any asset skill just like in a credit card or a personal loan.

CHAPTER 13: HOW TO PAY DOWN DEBT

A simple look online will show us that there are so many different ways that you can pay off your debt. And they are all going to work in slightly different manners. As long as they have you paying down your debt and ensuring that you don't take on new debt, without a bunch of risk in the process, then they are good options to work with. You can choose the one that makes the most sense to you.

We are going to spend some time, not looking at a specific plan that you are able to use to pay down your debt. Rather, we are going to focus more on the basic steps that you can do, no matter the kind of debt repayment plan you are using, to help make paying your debts off a little bit easier in the long run as well. some of the steps that we are able to use here include:

Stop with the New Debt

You are never going to get out of debt if you just keep adding to your debt number. It is always best to stop with the new debt and find ways to limit it as much as possible. Most people are not getting the right kind of training in how to handle money, and you may feel like it is impossible to get out of debt unless you are willing and able to go through the retraining process for your financial habits now.

You need to get right into the mix and make a stand against all of the marketers who are interested in trying to take your hard-earned money or offering you some easy financing as well. Keep in mind that while marketers are going to try to convince you otherwise, you really don't need more stuff to make you happy. What you need instead is financial peace of mind.

So, instead of having the temptation around and taking on more debt, cut up your credit cards so you can't use them. Sit down and come up with a budget, and then stick with it. Turn off the social media and the advertisements so that they are not able to control you any longer. This helps to limit the chances when you are tempted to purchase something that you do not need.

Rank the Debt Using Interest Rates

For this one, we are going to list out all of the debts that we owe, and list out the interest rate that comes with them. The highest interest rate needs to be put at the top of the list. That will be the one that you work on paying off first. Paying off the high-interest debt is going to be the key to what is known as the stack method of debt payoffs and can get that debt gone quickly.

There are other methods that work well too, but these often focus on motivational factors and can be a little bit slower at getting the work done. Interest is going to be a really powerful weapon, and right now, the banks or other companies are using it against you if you don't pay things off. Interest is going to increase the amount that you have to pay back in the end, and often we are not fully aware of how much that ends up being.

Let's say that we have a credit card that has a $10,000 limit on it, and there is 20 percent interest. You decide to just pay the minimum amount of $200 a month. In the end, it is going to take about 9 years and eight months (if you don't put any more money into it). This means that you are going to end up paying the bank $11,680 extra in just interest.

See if You Can Lower Interest Rates

In some cases, it is possible to lower your credit interest rates with the help of a balance transfer. You need to be careful with this one, but it means that you are going to move your debt to another bank, and they are going to offer you a lower interest rate to try and get your business.

If you are going to do this, you don't want to just jump right in. Make sure that you are going to actually pay the amount off rather than end up with two credit cards that are maxed out. And you should shop around to get the lowest amount of interest for the longest duration possible. Read through all of the terms and conditions that show up as well to make sure the bank doesn't have hidden fees or other issues that you need to be worried about.

Create Your Own Budget

This is where we are going to work on improving our own financial control. We need to bring out some pen and paper and write down what your total income is, after-tax, and then write down all of the expenses that we have. This includes any of the extras that you have and the minimum payments that you owe as well. We can cut these out later, but we just want a full look at it to start.

We can then look at all of the expenses that are there and rank them based on how important they are. Look at the items that are near the bottom of that list and determine if they are worth cutting to keep you financially stable. The objective here is to create a plan where you can get the expenses lower than the income.

You also need to go through and figure out how much you are willing to spend on all of the areas of your life. You can set aside amounts for eating out, groceries, rent, buying clothes, and more. Once you allocate that money though, realize that you are not allowed to dip into other areas, and you are done at that time. You may want to consider working with a fun account that will be there just for you to spend on something that doesn't usually fit into the budget. This allows you a bit of freedom without derailing the budget.

Even if your expenses are already below your income when you start, this doesn't mean that you can just stop here and call it good. You want to make sure that you can cut your budget down as much as possible. This allows you to make more money each month and throw it at your debt payments, making it more efficient and getting that credit score in line faster than ever.

Create Your Own Repayment Schedule

The first part that we need to focus on here is covering at least the minimum on all of the debts you have. If you miss anything, even if you are trying to pay off another debt faster, you are going to incur a lot of feed and more, and these can add up quickly. Make at least this payment each month.

Then, you take the debt that has the highest interest rate, and you will use the extra that is found in your budget and pay that extra towards that biggest debt. As you see, the official minimum payment goes down; you will be able to add the extra to your target debt. This will help you to really pay down the debt pretty fast, especially if you put any extra money towards that each month.

When that first debt is all done, then it is time to move on to the second-highest interest rate debt. With this one, you will take the minimum payment that you were doing before, along with the minimum payment that is available from the debt you paid off, and any extra you were paying. All of that goes towards the second debt, and that can be paid off in no time.

We continue this process, taking the extras that are used from one debt and throwing them at the next one on the line, with the payments getting bigger and paying things off faster as we go along. While the first debt may take some time to complete because you are also paying on all of the other debts, but the time you get to the last few, they will be paid off in no time.

Be Kind to Yourself

Keep in mind that paying off debt, even though it is so good for your credit score, is not something that you are going to be able to do overnight. During this process, which can be a long one, you will feel that your resolve is going to be tested quite a bit. You may have an emergency that happens, like a car breaking down, and you will have to change your plans a bit.

This is a normal part of life, and not something to get really frustrated about. The important thing to remember here is to not give up and revert to your old habits, or you will never get that debt paid off. Be kind to yourself when things in life happen, but don't give up. You will get those debts paid off in no time if you are willing to do the work.

The reason that we want to work so hard at paying down our debts and making sure that they don't stick around for a long period of time is that it helps us with our credit scores while freeing up more money to do what we want. When our utilization rates are lower because we pay things off, and we don't miss payments because the amounts are not as high as they were, then our credit score will go through the roof.

CHAPTER 14: WHAT IS A CREDIT SCORE?

Your credit score is a simple three-digit number used to judge your creditworthiness as a customer. It is calculated by using your credit history. From lenders to prospective employers and other financial institutions, various third parties use your credit score. It is used to determine whether you can repay your debts or not. The credit score can range from 300 to 850. The higher the credit score, the greater is one's financial stability. Fair Isaac Corporation is accredited with the creation of the credit score model. It is also known as FICO and is used by various financial institutions. There are a couple of other credit scoring models too. Still, FICO is the most popular and commonly used model these days. You can maintain a high credit score by ensuring you have a history of timely payment of bills and by maintaining a low debt level. There are various factors, which influence your credit score. A credit score is one of the key criteria evaluated by a lender while offering credit to prospective borrowers. A credit score of less than 640 is considered to be subprime. From a lender's perspective, the lower your credit score is, the higher the risk of default. So, the rates charged by financial institutions on loans increases as the credit score decreases. According to FICO, a credit score between 800 and 850 is believed to be excellent while the one between 300 and 579 is poor. The good news is regardless of what your credit score is, you can work on improving it.

Benefits of a Good Credit Score

The dependency on credit for making purchases is growing by the day in modern society. Good credit is no longer just used for securing a loan or even getting a credit card. The list of businesses using your credit score to determine their decision about extending their products or services to you is steadily increasing. In this section, you will learn about all the benefits of having a good credit score.

Interest Rates

The interest you pay is the cost of acquiring credit or borrowing any money. Apart from repaying the principal amount you borrowed, you must also pay interest to the creditor or the lender. The interest rate chargeable is influenced by your credit score. A good credit score means you can qualify for the best interest rate in the market. So, it directly helps reduce the finance charges on loans or credit balances. This, in turn, means you will be paying a low rate of interest and will be able to repay the debt quickly.

Qualify for Credit

Borrowers with a history of poor credit usually avoid applying for new sources of loans or credit because they were turned down in the past.

If you have a good credit score, it does not necessarily guarantee you will be approved for a loan, because other factors will be considered like your level of debt as well as income. However, an excellent credit score certainly increases the chances of approval.

So, if you are looking to secure a new source of credit, then you can apply for it confidently if you have a good credit score.

Power to Negotiate

When you have a good credit score, it gives you the power to negotiate a lower interest rate while securing new lines of credit. By leveraging your power to negotiate, you can make the most of all the competitive offers you get from other companies according to your credit score. On the other hand, with a low credit score, the lenders will be stricter and more rigid with the terms of loans. Also, the number of options available to you will decrease.

Borrow More

Your credit score and earning capacity determine your borrowing capacity. When you have a good credit score, lenders will be more comfortable allowing you to borrow more because of your history of prompt repayment. Even with a poor credit score, you will be able to borrow, but you might not qualify for higher limits.

Properties

These days, landlords have started to use credit scores while screening potential tenants. A poor credit score caused due to any previous evictions or outstanding rents can harm your chances of renting a property. A good credit score gives the landlords confidence about your ability to pay the rent on time and not default on rental payments. So, if you want less hassle while searching for a rental property, you must work on improving your credit score.

Car Insurance

Various companies that provide auto insurance use credit scores to determine the premium payable by policyholders. In the insurance circle, it is a popular belief that an individual with a poor credit score is going to file for more insurance claims. Therefore, they charge a higher premium for such people. With a good credit score, the chances of paying high rates of premium on auto insurance will decrease.

Cell Phone

A bad credit score can directly influence your ability to get a cell phone on a contractual basis. Cell phone service providers are often wary of all those who have a bad credit score. If pay-as-you-go plans hold little appeal to you, then work on fixing your credit score.

Also, if you have a good credit score, you might be allowed a little slack. You might not have to pay any security deposit while getting a cellphone on a contractual basis.

Utilities

The deposits payable on utility services can be anywhere between $100 and $200. It can be a costly expenditure while you are relocating. You might not have any plans of relocating right now, but if you do have to in the future, then a good credit score will come in handy. A good credit score means you do not have to pay any security deposit while transferring a utility service to a new location or while obtaining a new utility service.

You can certainly survive with poor credit, but it will prove to be rather expensive and difficult. By maintaining a good credit score, you can reduce your financial stress.

The Five Steps to Order a Credit Report

You can order your annual credit report online within a couple of minutes. It is certainly quite easy and is an important step you must follow while trying to repair your credit. You cannot work on repairing your credit score unless you are aware of the areas where you are lacking. For this, you will need your credit report. In this section, you will learn about simple steps you might have to follow for obtaining your credit report.

Identification

You will be required to provide certain basic identifying information for obtaining your credit report. The details you will be required to provide include your full name, current address, and date of birth. While providing your full name, you must also include your maiden name if you have any along with any different name you might have used in the past. You might also have to mention your previous address if you recently moved or have lived elsewhere in the preceding six years. Make sure that all this information is accurate while submitting a requisition for a credit report.

Provide the Social Security number

Identity theft is certainly on the rise these days. Once crooks manage to get your Social Security number, they can assume your identity. Therefore, it is but obvious that a lot of people are reluctant about providing this vital piece of information. If you are reluctant about doing the same, you will need to overcome this fear, especially if you are asking for your credit report. The credit bureaus use your Social Security numbers to keep track of your credit profile. While entering your Social Security number online, make sure that the site you are using is a legitimate one. A simple tip to keep in mind is to check for asterisks as you are entering the number. A fraudulent website will not show any asterisks, and if the site you are on does not show the same, then close the browser window immediately.

Provide Authorization

Before the website can provide your credit report, you will be required to confirm your identity as a means of authorization. Any person who has access to your basic identification information can easily obtain your credit report. To prevent this, you will need to authorize your position. So, you might be asked a couple of questions about your credit history like the name of the agency that issued your credit card or the lending agency that provided your home loan. Once you answer the security questions, the authorization will be complete, and you can obtain your credit report.

Credit Card is Required

You are legally entitled to receive a free credit report annually from each of the three leading credit bureaus in the U.S. If you are asking for your free report, then you must not be asked for any credit card information before the report is provided. However, you might have to pay certain charges if you are looking for any other service apart from this. Before you start giving out your credit card information, make sure that the website you are using is a legitimate one.

Basic Steps to Follow

Here are the simple steps you are required to follow to obtain an online credit report.

• Fill out the necessary details for personal identification like your full name, social security number, date of birth, and address.

• Place the requisition for a credit report.

• Complete the verification and authorization process by answering security questions.

• Generate your credit report online.

Follow these simple steps, and within a couple of months, you will have your credit report.

CHAPTER 15: HOW TO BOOST YOUR CREDIT SCORE OF 100 POINTS

You can in any case improve your FICO rating regardless of whether you can't get any negative things expelled, or on the off chance that you choose to sit tight for them to tumble off of your report normally. It's likewise imperative to deal with accumulations with consideration so you don't erroneously reset the date of the legal time limit.

Pursue these means as a major aspect of your far-reaching credit fix system to ensure you make the most of all things considered and dodge accidental difficulties that could cause enduring harm.

Survey Your Accounts in Collections

Start off by taking a gander at your ongoing accumulations. They have the most effect on your credit on the grounds that more up to date obligation is weighted all the more vigorously. Additionally, focus on the sort of obligation you're paying.

The medicinal obligation doesn't influence you to acknowledge as much as different sorts of obligations; so center around any non-therapeutic obligation first.

Attempt to make full installments since halfway installments can reset as far as possible for to what extent those records can stay on your credit report.

You can likewise attempt to arrange a settlement with the accumulation organization to pay short of what you owe. Simply understand that you may need to report the sum that was rejected as pay on your assessment form, which could bring about higher expenses and even a higher duty rate on the off chance that it knocks you into another level of pay.

Another issue with satisfying delinquent payment accumulations can happen if the gathering office goes about as though you haven't made any installment whatsoever. Maintain a strategic distance from this trick by getting installment understandings recorded as a hard copy and keeping duplicates of all reports identified with the record.

Keep on Checking Your Credit

When you've dealt with your records in accumulations, ensure those progressions are precisely thought about your credit report. It might take a month or two for the records to drop off, so hold up a little while before checking your report and your FICO rating.

In the event that you don't perceive any positive changes or the negative thing is as yet recorded, you should document a debate with the credit authority. For whatever length of time that you kept great records, you ought to have all the fitting documentation your requirement for a snappy debate process.

Quick Tips for Repairing Your Credit

Getting negative things erased from your credit report can have emotional outcomes on your financial assessment, however, it's a procedure that can take a ton of time.

In case you're searching for fast upgrades, there are as yet a couple of techniques you can utilize. Some are little fixes while others can at present have a major effect, so check the entire rundown to see which ones you can attempt today to fix your credit.

1. Lower Your Credit Utilization Ratio

The closer you are to maximizing your cards, the lower your FICO rating will be.

In this way, it bodes well that squaring away your equalizations on your charge cards can bring down your proportion and increment your score. Concentrate on maximized cards as opposed to those with low adjusts; thusly, you could see as much as a 100-point increment over a time of a couple of months.

2. Request a Credit Limit Increase on Credit Cards

On the off chance that you can't bear to satisfy the additional obligation to diminish your credit usage, regardless you get an opportunity for enhancements.

Call at least one of your charge card backers and request an expansion on your card limit.

You would prefer not to really charge anything else than you as of now owe. You essentially need to have a higher farthest point with the goal that your current parity comprises of a littler level of your accessible credit.

Here's a model. Let's assume you owe $5,000 on a card with a $10,000 limit. You'd use half of your credit. Yet, in the event that you got your limit up to $15,000, at that point your $5,000 equalization would just use 33% of your breaking point.

When deciding to your loan boss, it helps on the off chance that you've submitted normal on-time installments since your commencement with them. More than likely, they'll esteem client faithfulness enough to enable your credit to the line.

3. Become an Authorized User

Building your record as a consumer takes a great deal of time, however, there is an alternate way accessible. Locate a dear companion or relative who has long-standing, solid credit and request them to turn you into an approved client on at least one of their records. That Mastercard record will naturally be added surprisingly to your report completely.

There's a touch of hazard associated with this move: if your companion or relative quits making installments or conveys an enormous equalization, those negative passages will also be added surprisingly to your history.

In a similar manner, in the event that you rack up additional adjusts and don't help make any installments you're in charge of, the other individual's credit will wind up harmed. This can be an incredible strategy, yet it requires some alert.

4. Solidify Your Credit Card Debt

Another fast method to fix your credit is to consider getting an obligation solidification advance. It's essentially a kind of close-to-home advance that you utilize to pay the debt of your different Mastercards. At that point pay a solitary month-to-month balance on the advance.

Contingent upon your financing costs, you may have the option to get a good deal on your regularly scheduled installments by getting a lower advance rate. Shop around utilizing pre-endorsements to perceive what sort of rates you meet all requirements for and how they stack up contrasted with your present card rates.

Regardless of whether you make back the initial investment on your regularly scheduled installments, your FICO assessment will at present observe a lift since portion advances are seen more positively than spinning credit.

5. Get A Credit-Developer Loan

Small banks and credit associations regularly offer credit-manufacturer advances to enable people to fix their credit. When you take out the credit, the assets are stored into a record that you're not ready to get to.

You, at that point start making regularly scheduled installments on the advanced sum. When you've reimbursed the whole credit, the assets are discharged for you to utilize.

It might appear to be unusual to profit you can't spend, however, it's a path for the monetary establishment to feel ensured while you get an opportunity to substantiate yourself as a capable borrower.

When you effectively complete your installments and get the cash, the bank reports your installments as on-time to the credit authorities to assist your FICO rating.

6. Utilize Just a Little Segment of Your Credit Limit

"Credit use" is credit-represent the level of your credit breaking point you're utilizing. The sum you utilize powerfully affects your FICO assessment — just paying on time matters more.

Most specialists prescribe going no higher than 30% on any card, and lower is better for your score. When your Mastercard backer reports a lower equalization to the credit departments, your score can profit. Your score won't be harmed by past high credit usage once you've cut adjusts down.

7. Get a Co-Signer

In case you're experiencing considerable difficulties gaining admittance to credit, ask a relative or companion to co-sign an advance or charge card. This is colossal support: You're requesting that this individual put their credit notoriety on hold for you and to assume full liability for reimbursement in the event that you don't pay as concurred. The co-underwriter may likewise be turned down on the off chance that they apply for more credit later in light of the fact that this record will be considered in surveying their money-related profile. Utilize this alternative with an alert and be sure you can reimburse. Inability to do so can harm the co-endorser's credit notoriety and your relationship.

8. Pay On Schedule

Take care of your tabs and any current credit extensions on schedule, without fail. No single factor influences your financial assessment as much as your history of on-time installments. When you are reconstructing credit, you can't bear to miss an installment.

Late installments remain on your credit answers for as long as seven years, so these take more time to recoup from than some other credit slips up.

On the off chance that a few bills have just become delinquent, however, organize the ones where your record is as yet open. Gatherers may make the most clamor, yet they aren't your top need.

CONCLUSION

Fixing your credit is the best solution and should become more popular in the United States because I think it can really make a difference for a great number of people. Credit repair might seem complicated to some, and it definitely takes time to finalize, but nothing great is ever accomplished without a little bit of work. Also, there is no specialist that can claim that a credit repair done in one way or another has a 100% success rate. If they do, be careful with people trying to scam you for money while claiming they are repairing your bad credit.

The benefits of fixing your credit might reveal themselves over an extended period of time; however, by carefully doing all the steps describes here, you will eventually clear your credit and increase your chances of you ending up with increased scores on a credit application. It will also help you with finding a job, even though your credit is not entirely repaired. When someone is evaluating your credit report and sees the written statements and all the work you have put in for the process, it shows how responsible and preoccupied you are about your finances and says a lot about who you are.

9 781802 945959